WEATHER & CLIMATE

Be a Weatherman and... Explore

- Weather and Climate
- Seasons
- Weather Phenomena
- Precipitation
- Spectacular Sky Displays
- Clouds
- Wind and Wind Patterns
- Ocean Currents
- Weather and Climate Forecasting
- Weather Elements

WEATHER AND CLIMATE

What is Weather?

The weather is just the state of the atmosphere at any time, including things such as temperature, precipitation, air pressure and cloud cover. Weather describes whatever is happening outdoors in a given place at a given time. Weather is what happens from minute to minute. The weather can change a lot within a very short time. Weather includes daily changes in precipitation, barometric pressure, temperature, and wind conditions in a given location. Daily changes in the weather are due to winds and storms. Seasonal changes are due to the Earth rotating around the sun.

What is Climate?

Climate describes the total of all weather occurring over a period of years in a given place. Climate is the average weather usually taken over a 30-year time period for a particular region and time period. This includes average weather conditions, four weather seasons like winter, spring, summer, and fall, and weather disasters like tornadoes, storms, floods, etc.

Can you differentiate between Weather and Climate?

Climate is not the same as weather, but is the average pattern of weather for a particular region. Weather describes the short-term state of the atmosphere whereas climate gives the total description of all weather over a longer span of time.

SEASONS

Did you know?
There are no seasons in the grasslands of Savannah and hence the climate is determined by a rainy season in summer and a dry spell in winter.

Fall

Why do we have Seasons?

Since Earth is round and not exactly flat, the Sun's rays don't fall evenly on the land and oceans. Earth continually keeps on changing its position towards the Sun as it travels along its orbit. At certain times, we are closer to the sun and at other times we are further away. The Sun shines more directly near the equator bringing these areas more warmth. However, the polar regions are at such an angle to the Sun that they get little or no sunlight during the winter, causing colder temperatures. These seasonal differences are caused due to the slight imbalance of the earth's axis. All these seasonal changes determine the climate in several different regions of the earth.

Summer

Winter

Spring

WEATHER PHENOMENA

On Earth, common weather phenomena include wind, cloud, rain, snow, fog and dust storms. Less common events include natural disasters such as tornadoes, hurricanes, typhoons and ice storms. Almost all familiar weather phenomena occur in the troposphere.

Thunderstorm

It is a transient, sometimes violent storm of thunder and lightning, often accompanied by rain and sometimes hail also. A thunderstorm is formed from a combination of moisture, rapidly rising warm air and a force capable of lifting air such as a warm and cold front, a sea breeze, or a mountain.

What are the causes of thunderstorm?

Thunderstorms are caused due to large potential difference between cloud and ground. A thunderstorm is a cloud formation where large amounts of water undergoes a cycle of condensation, freezing and then re-vaporization as the currents of vapor within the cloud rises and falls. They usually seed in cumulonimbus clouds.

Cumulonimbus cloud

Did you know?
The fear of lightning and thunder is called ASTRAPHOBIA.

What is Lightning?

When liquid and ice particles above the freezing level collide and build up large electrical fields in the clouds, lightning is produced. It usually occurs during the thunderstorms. Lightning is an electric current. The temperature inside a lightning bolt can reach 50,000 degrees F.

Tornado

A tornado is a small, but very disastrous whirlwind that appears over the mainland. It is the violently spinning air column connecting the thunderstorm to the ground. When warm air rises upwards in the form of a spiral below a powerful thunderstorm cloud, it gains the spinning speed and rises upwards. They can move at speeds of more than 300mph and can suck up everything in their path.

Did you know?
In 1931 a tornado in Mississippi lifted an 83 ton train and tossed it 80 feet from the track.

What is a Gustnado?

It is a gust front tornado. It is a small and weak tornado that occurs along the gust front of a thunderstorm.

Amazing Facts

- Tornadoes can reach a wind speed of 500 kmph and hence can be very dangerous.
- Three out of every four tornadoes in the world occur in the United States.
- A tornado in Oklahoma on May 3, 1999 was the most destructive tornado in history causing over $1 billion in damage.
- Fujita Scale - The scale that measures the strength of tornadoes based upon the wind speed.

Hurricane

Hurricanes are the deadliest storms on the earth as these are powerful swirling masses of cyclonic wind, clouds and rain. Tropical whirlwinds or cyclones are referred to as hurricanes. Hurricanes are characterized by a low-pressure core capable of generating thunderstorms. They can wash away entire beaches, sink boats, pull trees right out of the ground and kill people.

What gives rise to the formation of Hurricane?

Hurricanes usually appear above the tropical waters when the temperatures are slightly high. This causes the enormous water to evaporate above the heated oceans. The water vapour starts rising up. The heat is released as moist air rises, during evaporation. Thus the condensation of water vapor fuels the formation of cyclonic windstorm.

The Eye

The center of a hurricane is called the "eye" and it can be up to 20 miles across. Surprisingly, the weather in the "eye" is calm with low winds and clear skies.

Eye

Amazing Facts

- The costliest hurricane of all time was Hurricane Andrew. Andrew struck Florida in 1992. The estimated cost damage was $26.5 billion.
- These whirlwinds are referred as 'hurricanes' in America, 'typhoons' in West Pacific, 'cyclones' in Indian ocean, 'willy-willy' in Australia.
- The world's worst hurricane that caused the highest loss of life took place in Bangladesh in the year 1970. The hurricane created a flood that killed more than one million people.
- The intensity of a hurricane is measured on the Saffir-Simpson Scale.

Waterspout

Waterspouts are most common over tropical or subtropical waters. They are of the nature of a tornado or whirlwind, that appears above the ocean and larger water bodies. It has funnel-like appearance. When this touches the surface of the water, water is pulled upwards inside the whirl. They sometimes rise up to a height of 450 metres in the sky. Waterspouts fall into two categories.

Fair Weather Waterspouts: Fair weather waterspouts usually form along the dark flat base of a line of developing cumulus clouds. This type of waterspout is generally not associated with thunderstorms.

Tornadic Waterspouts: Tornadic waterspouts are tornadoes that form over water, or move from land to water. They have the same characteristics as a land tornado. They are associated with severe thunderstorms.

Blizzard

It is a kind of snowstorm but accompanied with winds blowing at a minimum speed of 35 miles per hour. A blizzard can be very dangerous as it reduces the visibility and thus bringing everything to a standstill.

Supercell

A supercell thunderstorm includes a giant rotating updraft capable of producing tornadoes. Supercells are the strongest thunderstorms. In fact supercells are so large they show up on a satellite photograph in the shape of a tear drop. Most of the large tornadoes and giant hail events are spawned by supercells. The reason why supercells are the most severe is because of their rotating structure.

Downburst

It can be defined as the severe localized downward gust of air that can be experienced beneath a severe thunderstorm. These are the strong winds which move downward in a thunderstorm. There are two types of downbursts: microbursts and macrobursts.

Microburst: If the diameter of the downdraft is 4km or less than that, it is called a microburst.

Macroburst: If the diameter of the downdraft is 4km or more than that, it is called a macroburst.

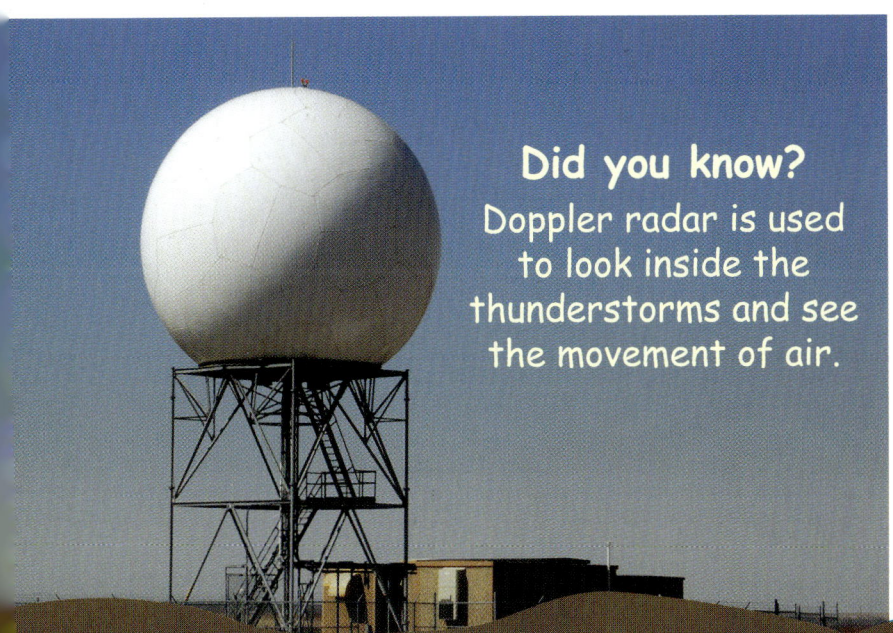

Did you know?
Doppler radar is used to look inside the thunderstorms and see the movement of air.

Interesting Fact:
On the 4th of July, 1977, a very strong and widespread downburst event hit northern Wisconsin with winds that were estimated to exceed 115 mph, which completely flattened thousands of acres of forest.

PRECIPITATION

Snow

Snow is frozen water. It is the precipitation falling from clouds in the form of ice crystals. It is made up of tiny, six-sided ice crystals, which form on dust particles inside very cold clouds. The crystals grow in size and join together. They become heavy and drop down through the clouds.

Why do we have Snowfall??

When a temperature in a cloud drops far below the freezing point, ice crystals are formed inside it. As ice crystals form, they collide with each other, become heavier and drop down on earth in the form of patterned snowflakes. No two snowflake shapes are ever alike.

Most beautiful forms of Nature-Snowflakes

The ice crystals always have six surfaces and six vertices but each snowflake is unique. Their form depends on the temperature, height and water content of the cloud.

Did you know?
No two snowflake shapes are ever alike.

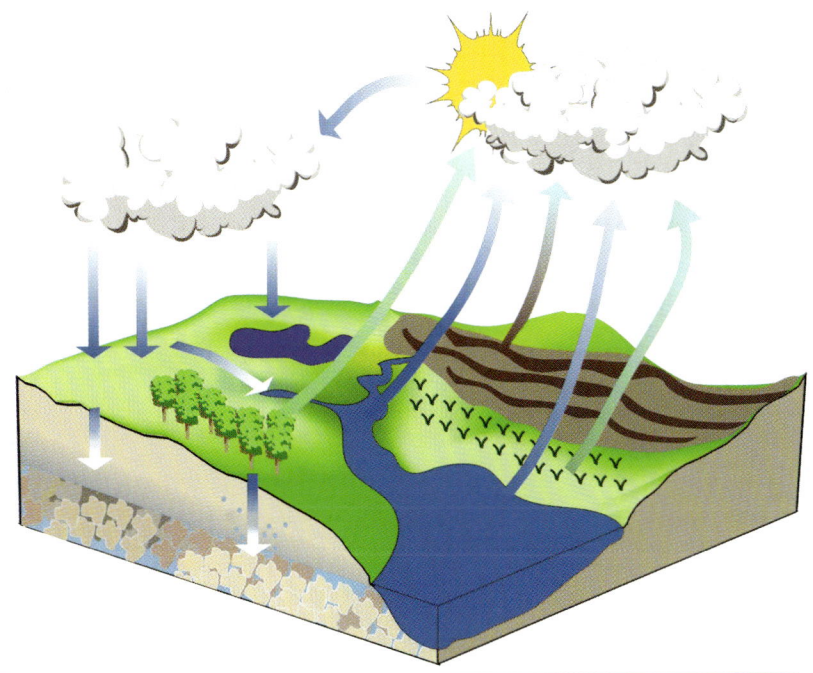

Rain

Rains are the drops of fresh water that fall as precipitation from clouds. It is a form of precipitation in which water falls back to earth as a liquid rather than solid.

What do you understand by RAIN CYCLE?

Rain cycle is also known as the hydrologic cycle. In this cycle, water evaporates from the ocean in the form of water vapor and eventually returns to land and sea in the form of precipitation. This cycle is the continuous circulation of water within the Earth's hydrosphere, and is driven by solar radiation. This includes the atmosphere, land, surface water and groundwater. The two processes responsible for moving the greatest quantities of water are precipitation and evaporation.

Drizzle

Drizzle is the light rain precipitation consisting of liquid water drops smaller than those of rain, and generally smaller than 0.5 mm (0.02 in.) in diameter. Drizzle is normally produced by low stratiform clouds and stratocumulus clouds.

Sleet

Sleet is wintry precipitation, and its exact definition depends on where you are. It is the partially melted snow. Sleet also causes moisture on roads to freeze and become slippery. Sleet forms when a raindrop or a snowflake partially melts as it falls through a layer of warm air higher in the atmosphere and turns back into ice as it falls through a deep layer of cold air at the surface.

Graupel

In a process known as accretion, ice crystals form instantly on the outside of the snow and accumulate on the original snowflake. The coating of these ice crystals on the outside of the snow is called a rime coating. The size of graupel is typically under 5 millimeters, but some graupel can be the size of a coin. Graupel pellets typically fall apart when touched or when they hit the ground. Graupel refers to precipitation that forms when supercooled droplets of water condense on a snowflake, forming a 2-5 mm ball of rime.

Ice Pellets

Ice pellets are a type of precipitation that is basically freezing rain refrozen. Ice pellets only fall in the colder months, since they need layers of air below freezing to be created. They are made up of ice and are translucent.

Freezing Rain

Freezing rain actually is rain falling while temperatures are just below the freezing point. Freezing rain is formed when warm air and cold air combine. This causes the rain to fall and freeze at the same time. Freezing rain is very dangerous as it turns roads into slick ice and damages the power lines and homes. It is important to note that freezing rain is in liquid form until it strikes a cold surface. The water droplets are super cooled and freeze on contact.

Frost

When the air near the Earth cools below its freezing point on a cloudless night in very cold weather, the water vapour converts into innumerable ice-crystals. This leads to the formation of a fine, silvery sheet of ice all over the trees, plants and meadows.

FOG

Fog is nothing more than a cloud that lies in proximity to the earth's surface. It often appears in the evening or at night when the warm and moist air close to the ground cools down. The millions of fine little droplets of water form the fog. When the visibility near the earth's surface is reduced to 1 km or less due to floating water droplets in the air, it is known as fog.

Hailstones

Hail is a form of precipitation which consists of balls or irregular lumps of ice (hailstones). Hail is pieces of ice falling from the sky. Hailstones on Earth usually consist mostly of water ice and measure between 5 and 50 millimeters in diameter. They form in very cold cumulonimbus rain clouds. Most hailstones melt before they reach the ground. Hailstorms are usually short and violent.

How are Hailstones formed?

Hail forms on condensation nuclei such as dust, insects, or ice crystals, when super-cooled water freezes on contact. Hailstones are usually from the size of a small pea to the size of a golf ball.

Did you know?

The largest hailstone ever recorded fell on 22nd June 2003 in south-central Nebraska, and measured 7 inches in diameter and 18.75 inches in circumference.

SPECTACULAR SKY DISPLAYS

Rainbow

How is a rainbow formed?

They are one of the most common but most spectacular sky displays. A magnificent rainbow often appears in the sky after violent thunderstorms. Rainbows are formed by the reflection and refraction (bending) of sunlight passing through raindrops. In heavy rains a double rainbow can often be seen. The sequence of a rainbows color is red, orange, yellow, green, blue, indigo and violet.

Fogbow

A fogbow is a whitish semicircular arc seen opposite the sun in fog. The fogbow is caused by sunlight refracting inside water droplets. The water droplets in a fog bow are much smaller as compared to the rainbow, and so the refractions aren't as precise. The tiny droplets of water cause a greater degree of refraction and thus form a white arc. These are sometimes also known as cloudbows.

Halo

A thick ring or circle of light that appears around the Sun or Moon sometimes is known as a halo. When the sunlight passes through small ice crystals, it is refracted and the halo is formed.

Moonbow

A moonbow is also known as a lunar rainbow. It is a rainbow produced by light reflected off the surface of the moon rather than from direct sunlight. Moonbows are relatively faint. They are always in the opposite part of the sky from the moon.

CLOUDS

Clouds

Clouds can be defined as a visible mass of fine and tiny droplets of water or frozen crystals suspended in the atmosphere. These droplets are so small and light that they can float in the air.

What are Clouds made up of?

The warm air full of water vapour goes up and cools down. As cool air can't hold much water vapour as compared to the warm air, the water vapour contained in it condenses to water droplets. When innumerable number of these water droplets form and accumulate, clouds are formed. When the sunlight strikes these clouds, the water droplets reflect back the sunlight. This gives clouds their white colour as they reflect all seven colours in equal amounts and hence the result is white.

Types of Clouds

There are different types of clouds. Weather experts call them by different names. Some are fluffy and white, while others are gray or dark. Clouds float at different heights, have different temperatures, and are made up of varying amounts of water, dust and ice. As clouds float through the cold air above the earth, they often hit areas where the air is warmer. The parts of the cloud touching the warm air then evaporate, leaving the cloud with a different shape. Winds blowing against the clouds also create new shapes. Clouds can be categorized into three main types based on their shapes and the process of their formation.

1. **Cirrus Clouds:** Cirrus clouds are the most common of the high clouds. These are found at high altitudes, above 20,000 feet. They are composed of ice and are thin and wispy clouds. Cirrus clouds are usually white and predict fair to pleasant weather.

2. **Stratus Clouds:** Stratus clouds are usually sheet-like in structure and uniform grayish clouds that often appear as continuous layers in sky. They resemble fog that doesn't reach the ground. These often produce drizzle.

3. **Cumulus clouds:** These are mostly rolled or rippled in appearance. Cumulus clouds are of medium height and are made up of ice-crystals and rain droplets. It is a convective cloud. These clouds can grow into more storm-like buildups including cumulonimbus.

WIND AND WIND PATTERNS

Wind

Air that moves from an area of high pressure to an area of low pressure is called wind. Whenever air is heated, it expands. This makes it lighter and the air rises. As the warm air rises, cooler air flows in to take its place. This movement of air is called wind.

Strong Wind

Light Breeze

Wind

Storm

Hurricane

Winds are an important part of our weather. Winds appear in many forms. Some are pleasant and useful and others are dangerous and devastating. Winds are very useful to us. It helps to dry clothes

hanging on the line, turn windmills, push sailboats through water and so on. However, there are harmful winds like tornadoes and hurricanes that are very strong and destructive.

Hurricanes and tornadoes are the deadliest storms on the earth as these are powerful swirling masses of cyclonic wind, clouds and rain. They can wash away entire beaches, sink boats, pull trees right out of the ground and kill people.

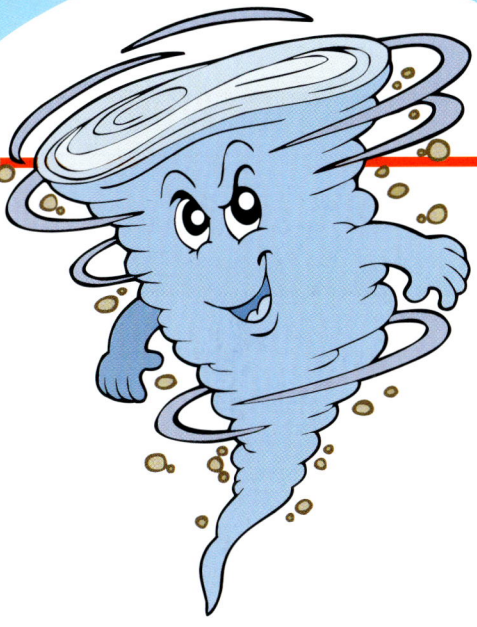

Did you know?
Without the wind, Columbus would never have been able to sail his ship and discover America.

Wind Patterns

Different parts of the Earth receive different amounts of heat. Near the equator, the Sun is overhead and heats the earth intensely. Near the poles, the sun's rays strike the earth at a low angle and so the heat is not so intense.

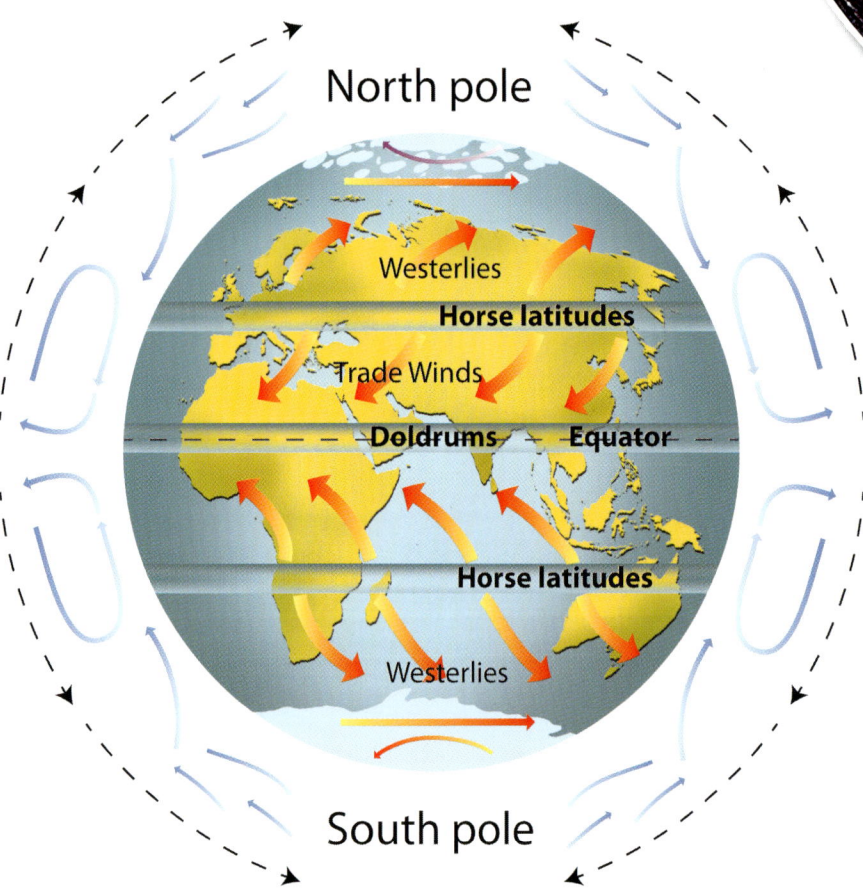

Trade Winds: Winds, caused by hot air rising upwards from tropical equator region and the cold air flowing from the earth's frozen regions into this space, flow in regular patterns. The streams of cool air are called trade winds.

Doldrums: The trade winds clash with each other along the equator. Doldrums are often caused at these regions. When the trade winds coming from the south and the north meet near the equator, they converge and produce general upward winds when heated. The doldrums are an area of calm weather also known as 'equatorial calms'.

Westerlies: A part of the air above the equator flows farther towards the poles. The rotation of Earth causes some winds that move toward the poles appear to curve to the east. Because winds are named from the direction in which they originate, these winds are called prevailing westerlies.

Land Breeze: At night, the above process is completely reversed. The land cools faster at night and thus the warm air above the sea rises upwards, pulling in air from the cooler land surface. This is known as land breeze.

Sea Breeze: During the day when the Sun heats the land faster than the sea. When the land surface is heated by radiation from the Sun, it expands and begins to rise. The rising air is replaced by the cooler air that draws in from above the surface of the sea and thus the wind blows from sea to land. This is known as sea breeze.

Did you know?
Land and sea breezes can be seasonal also. They are called the monsoons and are responsible for bringing heavy rains. These are abundant in the tropical coastal countries of the Indian Ocean.

OCEAN CURRENTS

El Nino and La Nina are opposite phases of the same cycle in the Pacific Ocean. El Nino and La Nina do not change with the regularity of the seasons. But they repeat on an average about every three or four years. They are the extremes in a vast repeating cycle called the Southern Oscillation, El Nino being the warm extreme and La Nina being the cold extreme.

What is El Nino Phenomenon?

The word El Nino is a Spanish word which means the "boy child" or "Christ child". A famous ocean current is the Humboldt Current which flows along the west coast of South America between January and March. Its cold water is rich in nutrients and many people survive on it. Around the Christmas, cold water is displaced by the warm water and this leads to many terrible climatic changes. This unusual warming of the surface waters of the eastern tropical Pacific Ocean is known as El Nino phenomenon. It causes changes in wind patterns that have major effects on weather all across the globe.

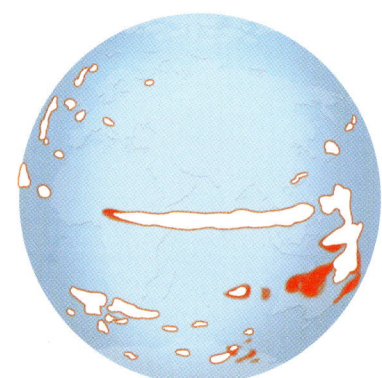

White and red areas show the El Nino phenomenan

What is La Nina Phenomenon?

La Nina is exactly opposite of El Nino. This stands for the "girl child" in Spanish. La Nina causes a widespread cooling of the surface waters of the eastern tropical Pacific Ocean. More appropriately, La Nina is the cold counterpart of El Nino, meaning sea surface temperatures in the tropical Pacific drop below normal. La Nina's form after some, but not all, El Nino's, and therefore occurs less frequently than El Nino.

Did you know?
Countries most affected by the variations in El Nino are Peru, Australia and India.

WEATHER AND CLIMATE FORECASTING

Scientists who study weather and climate are called meteorologists. They use different instruments like the windvane, thermometer, anemometer, rain gauge, barometer, etc to keep track of the following things:

- the temperature of the air
- the direction and speed of the wind
- the change in air pressure
- moisture in the air
- the clouds
- the amount of rainfall.

Meteorologists also have developed some sophisticated equipments, like Doppler radar and supercomputers, which give more specific and clear results. But many of them still rely on old-fashioned sky watching.

There are weather satellites going around the earth. Their cameras take pictures of clouds, the land, eyes in the sea storms, tornadoes and hurricanes. This information helps weather forecasters know about the weather. The network of five satellites called 'metstats' provide a weather watch for the whole world. You can often see metstat pictures on television weather forecasts.

Did you know?
Nexrad stands for "NEXt generation weather RADar", which is a nationwide network of 120 Doppler radars.

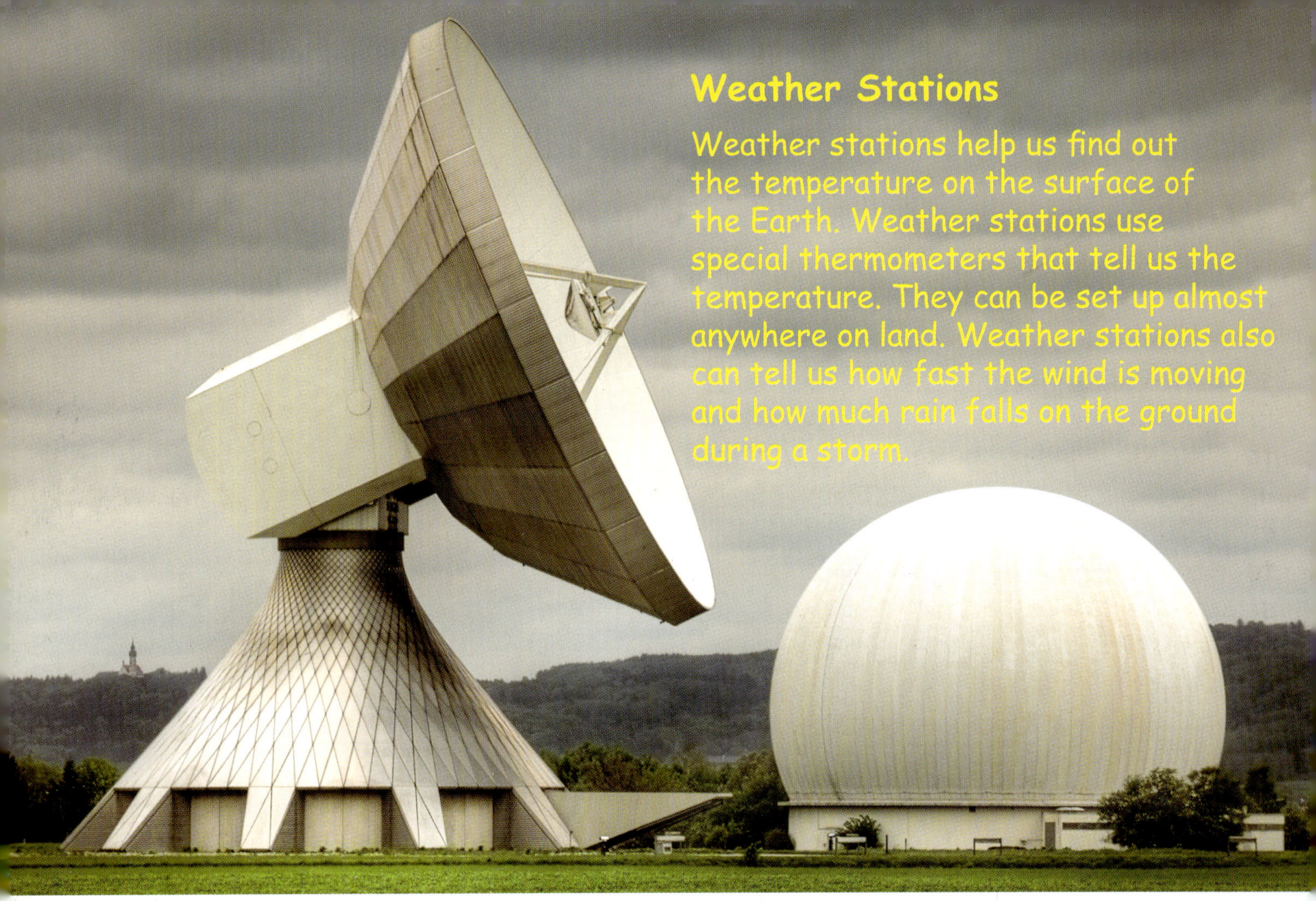

Weather Stations

Weather stations help us find out the temperature on the surface of the Earth. Weather stations use special thermometers that tell us the temperature. They can be set up almost anywhere on land. Weather stations also can tell us how fast the wind is moving and how much rain falls on the ground during a storm.

Weather Symbols

Weather Maps and Symbols

Weather forecasters make use of all the information they gather to make weather maps.

Weather Map

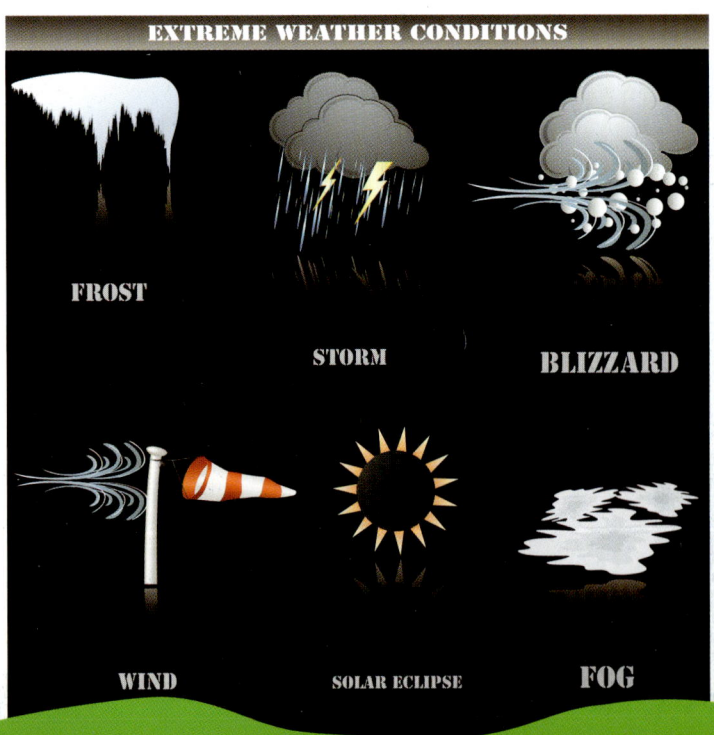